Contents

Contents

Contents

Contents

Contents

Prologue

Do you love poetry? I do. I love how poetry takes me places. I love how it conveys images from words and phrases, or even how it renders sounds and silence visible.

Do you believe in love? I do. My poetry recounts how we have always seen, felt, and experienced love—its presence or absence, whether glorious or frivolous.

I remember writing my very first poem when I was twelve years old. I wrote about nature, trees, and how—for me—these are symbolic of love. Sadly, as ephemeral words could be, I no longer possess or recall the exact written piece, which my dear grandfather so cherished.

Nevertheless, my love for poetry grew stronger and eventually took over me—my hand, my heart. Not only did I write more since then; I learned throughout the process as well. In fact, after countless revisions and over a decade of looking back, I now realise that I actually 'have written' and that I can truly write.

This book of personal souvenirs will take you through twelve years of love—a gripping feeling, an indescribable emotion, one state of being that you and I can only try to put into words but never really understand. Sharing the pages with other talented, youthful writers from different parts of the world, I feel deeply touched simply knowing that in loving poetry I am never alone.

As long as love exists and endures, we write.

K J C A
3 July 2012

I

manifestos

A Futile Lament

K J C A

Restless. stymied. dejected.
Because I am insignificant
and you are my entire universe
you are my entire universe
you are my entire universe.

And you conspire to devour me
until I submit to your will
and lose myself.

2007

Aquilae

YEN OOI

To view the world from afar
To accept what is seen and not mar
With subjective ideologies that burden the human race

To learn to be individual
Accepting things that are factual
Without enforcing representation through cultural malaise

To be free and alone
Not to worry or to hone
Instincts, practices or superstitions on the surface

To respect everybody
But not rely on anybody
Not to love or to hate, but be neutral to every face

To not fear
but listen and hear
Every opinion, insult, compliment, says

To be able to see
That the ability to flee
Nurture, feed and struggle, is the ultimate grace

To be humbled by the stars

Marenui

JAMES TREMLETT

The green and purple miles of seaweed
run high on southern shores.
Sifted in the memory
with dawn's coolnesses and pingao underfoot
shoots the sharp salt tang of kelp.

E hine,
below the meniscus
as the bright shafts sink their silver
between the fishes
and the stones, as the waters envelop
the limbs of crab and swimmer,
may we be conscious only
of te moana, the liquid that binds
between the gulfs of oblivion
shrimp, whale, shadowy albatross;
sand, alga, lobster;
human lovers, light.

Through the darting famished schools
flow muscular kahawai,
ethereal eels,
and this is te aroha:
not the lightnings of skin
or words, but the sharpness
of kina and kelp, the long
exultations of sharks.
It is sung in the salt, in the hot rush of blood
by choirs of plankton,
the multitudinous ones,
by the rays that glide and judge like angels,
by all we are, and are not,
suspended
in the violent caress of the tides.

Upon these remoter sands
where the pale towns hold only barrenness
against the deep, on your lips
is the olive scent of kelp,
the golden fertility of salt,
the liquid maritime dawn.
In the depths
far from storm and encroaching net
still you remain:
soft, persistent,
as the waves that whisper always
in my veins.

The seaweed thunders in my dreams.

I Wished I was the Sea

MARTIN VIDANES

I wished I was the sea,
And I did become it.
Coming and going upon the shores of my waking
At the steady cadence of the moon.

The winds stir me,
And push me from my vastness.
The sun evaporates my feelings
To breathe storms upon the earth and sea.

I wished I was the sea,
A vast and ever-deep hollow.
Weightless and heavy;
Bowing down to the whims of the moon

Who so distantly beckons and declines.
Pulling and pushing at my inanimateness.
Without a care alluring me into the night.
I wished I was the sea.

Drowning away the sorrows of my waking.
Burying deeper the whispers of yesterday.
Wishing I were the shore, or the sky,
Ever moving and ever still.

A Night Without You

JACEE ABARRIENTOS

Brightly, the moon glows
Across the velvet sky
Everywhere its light touches
Leaves a wake of divine silver

The stars twinkle, smile and dance
Oblivious, how much I adore them
Here I lay wishing, wishing
I could just as strongly entrance

Wonderful, how beautiful the night is
I turn, roll, sigh and squirm restlessly
Unrest, discomfort as my eyes fly in all directions
Searching, needing, missing, crying out for you

Even in the darkness of my eyes wide open
Your face, is still and always will be what, I seek
Even in the loud, deafening silence of my room
Your voice, is still and always what my ears yearn to hear

Even in the bleak scents of my surroundings
Your scent, loving and familiar, I long to inhale
Even in the unmoving warmth of my bed
Your embrace, soft and careful, I'd die for to feel

Beautifully cruel is this night, enchantingly merciless
It leaves me dazing, staring off into oblivion
Wishing for you, my love, my purpose
With its glory, the night hides the pain momentarily

Yet again I'd find myself
Crumpling, caving in and breaking down
My heart tightens, suffering in these long hours
Finding nothing but emptiness as I can only withstand so much

Again, my chest heaves as my heart tightens
Knowing that this night will go on too long
I stare up at the stars and the moon, with a hand
On my heart, tears threatening to spill from my eyes

Yet believing we're looking at the same sky
My heart beating in time with yours
Now you're never too far, even just for a while
As we look up at the same sky, the same stars and the
Brightly glowing moon.

The Galaxies that Surround Us

AIMEE BETTINA BAUTISTA

A kaleidoscope of stars in a variety of colors
All unfolding between me and you
I shall not desire to be in the arms of another
Only my love for you is true.

Hearing your heartbeat, every note;
Smelling your strong yet delicate scent,
And as your arms envelop me and hold me close,
You keep my soul's sanity unbent.

I feel there is a light that centers you and me
And it is what makes our souls unite.
It sparkles and shines for the entire world to see,
And it spreads out to give the world a bite.

The spirals of constellations and dashes of blue
Glitter like your breathtaking eyes.
My heart starts to race in your calm ocean of dew,
And nonetheless you never fail to surprise.

So as galactic bodies surround us tonight,
Then you let your lips linger softly
Your beautiful face is a magnificent sight,
And charm me into you enchantingly.

Melodies and Promises

BEVERLY LUMBERA

If you wear an illusion, I will make it real.

You were unexpected. Right now, you seem so surreal to me.
Like the beautiful images of Kuekenhof, Bonn, or Portillo.
They all look like something that cannot exist in this world.
Like something that can only be built in dreams,
      meant for the heavens, or for a world beyond Earth.
But the fact is, they exist—real, palpable, and concrete.
All of their wonders can be seen, touched, heard, smelt, and felt.
And I want you to know that it's the same with you.

Must you seize my world by storm.

I can see you.
      And your sunshine of smile that pierce through my loneliness.

I can smell you and your wonderful cologne that sticks perfectly
      to my skin.
      You smell just like what I imagined you'd smell like, possibly
      even better.

I can touch you.
      And your hands that fit so well in mine.
      And your shoulders which are unbelievably the opposite of
      puny which I thought they would be.

I can hear you.
      And the sound of your voice just brings happiness into my ears.
      That perfect tone which never fails to soothe and calm my
      fearful heart.

And yes, I can feel you. And everything of you.

I give myself in sweet surrender, my one and only love.

It frustrates me that I cannot do everything that I want to do.
Because fate is tricky.
And there is only so much that the human form can consume.
I'm afraid that if I let you in too early,
> you would just be stirred into all the uncertainties and
> confusion that I am likely to encounter in the way.
So until then, I hope that you can hold on to a promise.
> —to something that I also put my heart into.
That someday, we would go to all the beautiful places
> including those that we will create for our own.
And under the loving stars,
Or with the peace of the sun or the gentle calm of the wind,
Or with the soft green grass, or under the romantic full moon,
We will kiss.
And every second shall last forever.
Because you are mine. And I am yours.

I love you in a place where there is no space and time.

I Was Never A Sonnet, But I Was Yours

GINX PETTERSON

I love you without knowing why, when or from where*
I simply feel for you with all of me
No other emotion would ever compare
All of which my heart beats for thee

An arrow from cupid's silken bow
Is powerless under this stream of sunlight
There is no remedy for love but to love more
And fulfill one's yearning delight

Yet trails of crimson litter where brightness should be
From the agony of a steady beating broken
I had cared too much, too blind to see
To understand the pain unspoken

I love you without knowing why, when or from where
I simply feel for you with all of me
But I regret all which I could but did not share
The hopelessness of what could have been we

---

* after Pablo Neruda
  Sonnet XVII (English translation by Stephen Tapscott, 1986)

lost & found

FILAMOR SONGCO

my heart wandered...
like the prodigal son
and yet returned
to the embrace of his father

my heart wandered...
like odysseus
and yet fought his way back
to his home, ithaca

one day
my heart wandered...
alas, it never returned
but someone found it

give it back, i said
he smiled and took my hand
no, he whispered
take mine instead.

Captured

MM MERILO

My heart, it beats
Like the second hand
Of a very old clock:
So slow, so heavy,
So empty of energy.
My hands, they sway
Like tattered red ribbons
Blowing away in the air:
So weak, so flimsy,
So empty of grace and beauty.
My feet, they step
Like old wood,
A cane:
So graceless, so stiff
So dull and rigid.
Your eyes, they stare
And fuel my heart
'Til it pumped and pumped
And I felt my flowing blood.
Your sweat, it sears
My skin and burns my veins,
'Til it ate away my fears,
And set my soul on fire.

Can you

YEN OOI

A life within
with a soul, nurtured
escaped from this world
without even saying hello

A brave soldier
Quiet, calm, loved
Leaving in the night
before he could be found

Two hands entangled
grasping for strength
to overcome the pain
Thankful for the other
holding on to a memory
a feeling, an emptiness
Palm in palm
reminding the other
that they are here
now.

Darkness coming
Life is going
I'm dying, can you save me?
Light is shining
Love my breathing
I am living can you feel me?

[He]

J O S E   P A U L O   R.   L U I S T R O

[He] no longer sees the

[Ne]ed for attachment

[Ar]med with the conscious thought

That he's noble enough to exist alone.

Light Matters

LAKSMI PAMUNTJAK

All he ever talks about is the light.
In giving me a book about a writer's
retreat to the homes of Capadoccian
monks, I suppose he also expects me
to think about the light that shines on
certain stones on certain mornings.
Sure, I say, but the colour of white
is night. It is not the sun that guides
you to white. It is moonlight on stone.
He considers this, then suggests that
I should pay more attention to Anatolian
mornings, for there is a tintinnabuli to
such brightenings, hazel and silver
birches edging forward,
water fowls moving stepwise.
When said writer dies not a month
since he gave me the book,

he quietly goes to pieces.

Then he sits down to an obituary

of the sort that would make the dead

writer and Narcissus himself blush.

While he weeps in his own Virgilian hell,

I keep coming back to the railway of light

that fell across my chest that afternoon;

each time his eyes rested on the two bells on

each end, those soft and yielding summits,

I wonder whether he was actually savouring

the peach pill-boxes of a building in the 6th;

or whether he was tonguing, in his mind's

eye, the milky ovals next to the Rapunzel

tower. I wonder when he looked at me

whether it was my light that he saw,

or whether it was the light around me—

the one that had nothing to do with me.

Wiltshire, England

II

nemesis

Pen and Paper

Words relentlessly plummet from the enormous sky
plunging wildly into this starving, thirsting funnel
mixing with trickles of sweat, tears, and blood
concocting a potent fluid inducing madness.
I will paint the bleak horizon with fresh ink
and count the blots and traces of naught
to relinquish the unspoken truths in me
that tomorrow I will no longer recall.
I will spew utterances unheard of
to betray my congested heart
and fill up the empty spaces
in my mind, in between
words and soliloquies.
My poor reasoning
commands me
to just falter,
to recover,
to love
you.

Overdose

Like an innocuous drug
your kiss seeps into my lips,
blood surges beneath my skin,
my heart stops. breathless

You clasp my cold hands
cold, cold unfeeling arms,
scathing unforgiving wounds
wrestling with my numbed senses
forcing me to collapse.

If I take too much of you, will I live?
Your prescription proves too strong
a remedy for my convulsing heart.
If I take too little, will I survive?
Refusal is the next best thing
when strength escapes my senses,
when my mind stops to function,
when you leave me no choice.

I too, can feel!
I need that drug, your feisty antidote
sustain me with your innocuous dose
feed my mind with stimuli, kiss me again!

Resuscitate me.

Restore my sanity.

You are my guilty pleasure.
Your innocence revives.

For crying out loud

Can you hear me?
(Screams loud utterances.)

Now, can you hear me?
(Curses more.)

I repeat—can you hear me now?

I am mad, not in love,
but I am, with you.
I could produce sounds and curses
unimaginable, unintelligible to you
I could clench my fists in total restraint
or mindlessly, recklessly throw my body
until we collide head-to-head,
eye-for-an-eye, tooth-for-a-tooth.
I could articulate strings of vocabularies
and irregular verbs and phrases
you ought not to hear or know at all.

I am mad, not in love,
but I am, with you.
I am a master of sarcasm, an expert
of irony, wit, and judgment
and I have a right,
as much as
I have some left.

Can you just listen?
Just hear me out, I cry, listen to me—
I do not want to hurt you, see?
I just want to be heard, you see?
I neither asked too much nor too little,
I am mad, not in love,
but I am, with you.

(Yells.)

Bloodgame

Erratic.
Deep breaths and gasps
of cold, bitter air
sharp terror written on a face
Arms struggling,
claiming precious life
stained and fouled of
the thickness of deepest red
Hands that shuddered
in disbelief and guilt
attempting to wash the misdeed
of conceit and retribution
but failed, like many times
failed.

Reverberating bellows,
undulating banners and words
to resurrect precious life
to claim the act as pure
to assert justice in remorse—

These do not allow
the thickness of deepest red
to pay for the dark game
to deny the act
to return and revive justice

Hands once stained
rise and clench into hypocrisy
embodying the very name
of the blinded beast.

Desensitizing the senses

Deny me the taste of your garish promises
offer me sweetly your bland, flavorless scent
stir my ears with tongues of fire and fury
move me, again.

Your presence brings light
and the absence of taste and smell
you are the presence of silence
the absence of cold
touch me, again.

You are the absence of sanity
and the presence of yearning
the absence of thoughts
the presence of emptiness
the absence of answers
and the presence of love.

Nemesis

Your vision
captures hues, grains and textures,
reveals distorted compositions and disturbing montages.

The thin film at the surface of your eyes
is parched
and the thirsting soul beneath your pale skin
envies the seemingly endless watery streams
that flow in your mind.

While you sleep,
your body awakens vivid dreams and mysterious stigmas
your innermost desires melt into purées of colors—

reds, scarlet and crimson,
blues, cobalt and indigo,
yellows, grays,
and jet black.

One day,
as you wake up,
while you stare adamantly at the dreamy glare
of the afternoon sunrise,
of solid concrete and plastic skyscrapers,
of attractive eyes, unrecognizable faces, mutable sights,
of your reflection in front of the mirror—

You will see me and we will try again.

Grit

Each time you drive yourself mad
through miles of endless winding roads
cutting across rocks and mountains
curling around unnamed forests
she is the reason you are lost.

Each time you drive yourself mad
through miles of endless winding roads
cutting across columns and skyscrapers
turning around posts and stations
he is the reason you are lost.

Speed Limit

Each word that you don't speak
ticks
as I count the seconds and minutes
that stretch like roads and highways,
as I hum a muffled tune off the top of my head—
I'll sing that one for you some other day.

Yes, I meant to count
because I've got nothing else to do
whenever I'm beside you,
whenever you gave me no choice
but to measure the distance we've covered,
but to look out for signs that lead to you,
but to give up 'cause I'm tired.

I can measure
distance in miles, time, and streaks of light
time in seconds, heartbeats, and silence
and space in unusual places where we've met.
But I cannot measure—

the distance between you and me

the time I've spent in reckless dreaming

the gap you left in me.

You went past like a speeding light,
when I pulled over, you were still there
when I looked out, you were gone
when I closed my eyes, you were still there.

L. S. S.

Tired of running away from the groove and the crowd
the strobe lights and sounds,
the scratching so loud,
I glanced at my stiff hands—

2:17 a.m.

I dragged my feet, dragged myself,
shoes scratching on the floor,
kept dragging myself, dragging my feet—
my bed is just a taxi away.

"Just take me home. I want my bed, my pillow now."

Lights suddenly took speed—
faster and faster the lights dashed past me,
dashing like moonbeams.

Stop.

Staccato.

Message sent.

Heard my name so suddenly
I heard it right then and there
I dropped my phone into my pocket.
Batteries drained and empty.

I suppose he got it right.
I suppose she'll get it right.
A couple of lovers, a few notes,
a couple of birthdays, a few jokes,
a couple of greetings, a few ads.

Kept repeating a line or two
Over and over, I think of you
Over and over again, I think of you
Again and again, I think of you.

Stop.

"Keep the change."

I jumped off the cab,
with a voice still singing in my head like an echo.

An echo.

Ah, my bed!
I glanced at my stiff hands—

2:17 a.m.

CCTV*

MARTIN VIDANES

Let's play a game.

I spy. I spy a lens cap.
it covers my view. I cannot see
I do not know where or how you are.

But the recording is on.
And as I wait for the visual,
I can hear the reverberations of voices,
and other sounds, and yours.

I tilt, I turn, I twist
I fathom in the darkness,
watching over you, like some distant lover
that you forgot you installed.

But I cannot see you
Not when you do not want me to.
Not when you don't remember me,
Not when the *real* cameras are watching.

I hear the words, and the sounds,
and the dissipating light
I feel the electricity surge through me, when he speaks.
But I cannot defend you

Not when you don't want me to.
Not when you don't remember
That I'm always willing to watch over you.
Maybe I still love you.

---

* after KJCA

Admit One

Outside, I skillfully escaped curious glances,
swept through the unmoving crowd,
looked for you, recognized your face,
saw you smile.

Inside, you pressed my hand tightly, carefully,
as if what we have is real, whatever that means.
As if our fingers match, they fit like locks
and our hearts are keys, our minds are doors.

But in case you failed to notice—
I was first to take your hand
Whatever I felt right then and there,
I longed to tell, but my doors just shut.

Why does every time feel like the first time?
whenever we share this unpredictable quiet
around us, we feel as if time bends
for us in this mindless act, this scene,
one, two, four, several times.
Hands on you, feeling your heartbeat
Now, what do you feel?
What do you think?

Please, I told myself,
don't fall again, not this time
not when the time is not right, not ever.
But I want you now
more than ever, I see, I feel
just for this moment, I matter.

The Ballerina

My heart was walking me home last night
through empty streets and cold alleys
through thick and thin, and fleeting clichés
when I saw this moonlit sky,
this coloured photograph.

I took it
as a sign, a comforting vision
between windy breaths and chilly blows,
then saved it in my pocket,
skipped and smiled.

Then, from some invisible cloud up there,
a letter fell,
gently gliding like a delicate feather
or a downy petal—no,
a butterfly—
signed, sealed, sent by you.

Where did you come from,
why are you here?

I am the ballerina in your dreams.

Rain Suit Skating

Hurriedly, he got to the mall
bright eyes staring, big eyes amazed
swirling people, swooping skaters
where else can he fix his gaze?

Lured by the fairies' exquisite ballet
enticed by dainty dancing elves
He got himself in the freezing carnival
what an unusual ball!

Without a robe, a coat or jacket
He put on a rain suit instead—
well, outside it had just rained
and the gala was like a freezer.

He blushed,
knowing his suit was a little wrong
yet he threw himself into the ball
and gazed at his stunning reflection
at the frozen glass, the crystal bed
below him sparkling.

This dance happens to be my favorite,
a breezy display of glee and me—
as I remember that once I've been
wearing a rain suit skating merrily.

Left Side

Like a pinpricking light
to a moth coming from nowhere—
Warm. Magic.
Like a drop of water
to dry soil, barren and dead—
to feel life once more.

Who are you?
sitting to my left
right after I closed my heartdoor
leading to my yesterday
right after I let go of the chain
that bound me to a love
that lingers in the past
but exists no more now.

Tell me your name
but don't let me hear you say it
for I am an easy fool
and I might plant seeds in my head
tomorrow will never bloom.

How do I avoid you?
Now that I already see my reflection
in your eyes, wide open.
please hold my hand
but let me not feel your grasp
for I might end up
as the moth, entranced
circling and circling
until the flame breathes to me
and I burn, inside out.

A mindless recount

I have three things to say.

One.
I admit, yes,
I was a fool for you.
Who can tell who really made the first move?
It won't matter now, it never did, forget about it.
But you chose to tell, you brought me there,
and silly me, I fell for each word,
everything that came from your lips.
Ah! Those lips!

Two.
I admit, yes,
I fell for you but I never told you,
you don't have to hear me say it.
You just have to notice, you just have to feel—
that's what our hearts are for.
Or perhaps, you were too busy,
singing, dreaming, playing around
and I grew tired of waiting.

Three.
Maybe, I'm hurt
maybe you're not.
Just how do you expect someone like me
to sit back, relax, and wonder
what the hell happened?
Where did you go, what about me?
How about the little promises
we were meant to keep?

There's more to say,
more to hide, more to feel,
but I've just got three words today.

Move, please, move

Sometimes, people do not see.
At times, they do not move.
They tend to ignore and stand still
without knowing what moves.

Like today—
I've seen people without eyes, without hands,
I've seen some who choose to whisper
and I know they couldn't hear as well.

I walk and run and move about
and I see countless faces and facelessness
garbled sounds and white noise pierce my ears
as I force my mind to look.

Move, please, move
so I can see you from where you stand
Speak aloud, please, speak!
So I can hear you and recognize your face
and remember your name, and believe in you.

Move, please, move!
My innards are exposed, exhausted!
I have the right to demand what I need—
I need to know, I need to feel.

Madman

Sometimes I hear the clock tick,
sometimes I don't.

Other times,
it ticks so loud,
louder than heartbeats rushing.

Whenever I'm alone
in a quiet room,
in a room other than my own,
in your room,
in a room other than our own,
I keep shutting out time,
I stare at the stark white walls
and those glossy glass panes that arrest
the solid state of our viscous words.

Haven't you noticed?
Time seems to unfold too slowly at the start,
at the very start where seconds stretch like minutes
and minutes stretch like hours,
but
towards the end,
it chases us like a mad unknown
to the finish line that we never actually reach.

Before we run out of time and sand,
If only for you, I shall never finish this piece,
I'll offer you madly a heartbeat's skip,
as if a single beat in time will never cease.

You said, you said.

I tried to call you
but there's no answer.
Only if I could make my way
through the other end of the line
to see what you're up to
to know if you're really not there
to know if you're trying to
ignore me. Yes, ignore me.
I won't understand.
I'll just keep calling.

The crack of your voice
I can hear so suddenly
your way with words
I suppose would capture me
vulnerable, unprepared.
Making me believe all's done,
everything is going well,
forcing me to forget, to not mind
the open wounds you've caused me
driving me wild without my consent.
making me believe everything
you said, you said.
I realized I was wrong
although I am not
just because you said.

Appeased.

After a few months of make-believe,
several erratic days,
hours of missed sleep,
minutes of breathtaking encounters,
seconds of loving,
I choose to move on.

I recall telling you
that time does not exist,
that time is not real.

How strange—
right now, I yearn to go back
and revive the time
we've profusely wasted
and stolen from each other's arms.

Then again, I recall
our first time;
when you told me—
It was all well worth it.

Yes, it was all well worth it.

I fear

this torment,
utter disillusionment,
life imprisonment,
my empty bereavement.

I fear
the departure of love,
faith, hope, and truth,
thus the unfolding of woe,
and the dearth of my spirit.

I fear
that luminous moment
when no else will stand for me
stand by me, stand up for me,
please, understand me.

Only you can tell me

But you cause my world
to stop, halt, freeze
as if I'm waiting
for an answer
to make me realize
who I am, and who I am not
to you.

The truth shall lead me
to you or otherwise
But I'll take the risk—
so I may put myself in place
or retreat, or start again.

a 'French window' in Paris (4e quartier)

After Twelve Months

After twelve months—
let's not call it a year lest we regret our sense of time—
your messages still fill my broken phone
with letters in lower case, and repeating syllables,
elated punctuation marks, and crazy umlauts,
spaces between words, and spaces between lines.

Those spaces,
trifle as they may "seem",
we take them for granted—
you and I; that's what I meant by "we".

Those spaces,
they stretch like long days and endless nights,
they endure months and seasons of solitude,
they keep your secrets out of sight.

Beyond my sight, wherever you may be,
despite the space between us that spans years and oceans,
You happily add another twelve months,
you celebrate, you undoubtedly live, you finally move on.

(Belated happy birthday.)

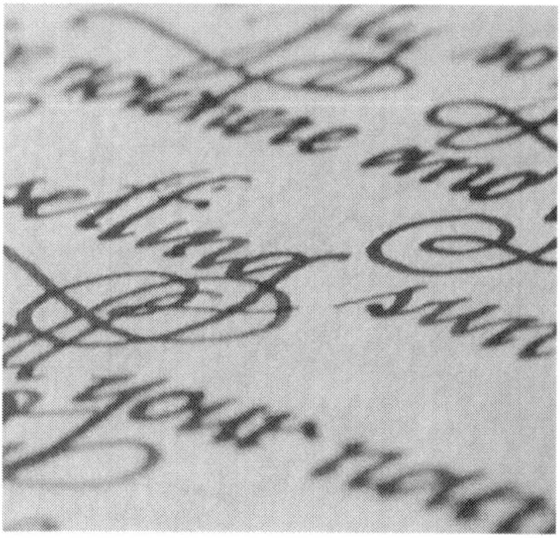

A Muted Libretto

Have you ever noticed
how time flies, how silently it fades away?
you were supposed to wait, stand still and wait
yet here you are, ready to start again
and here I am, savoring our last song,
our last chorus and refrain.

I hear your voice when I'm alone
you sing to me in the middle of the night
I see your eyes, they smile as sweet as your kiss
you whisper hushed words and sounds to my lips
I listen . . . I hear your laughter,
I feel your warmth, your arms, your heart,
your life, your future, everything about you.

Now, these thoughts,
these things, these feelings, these reminiscences
they linger, they persist in my mind.
dancing circling wallowing in my memory.
Stay with me, come back to me,
your words are sweet promises that lull me to
sleep deep slumber

> *I know,*
>
> *I can never spend more than a lifetime*
> *or another thousand years by your side,*
> *memorize your face for the rest of time*
> *recall your name when my memory fails*
> *or remember your words when my heart ceases.*

My heart is twisted, woven into my soul
one by one my senses lose control and let go of you—
your sound, your fingerprint stains,
your scent, your kiss, your enchanted gaze.
And in pure silence, I tremble in fear and yearning
for I know how it feels to lose you, how it burns.
And as I helplessly wait for that treacherous time,
you will sing a song, you will take flight
in the middle of the night, while I sleep, my eyes closed,
or while I am awake and trapped in frivolous daydreams.

Listen now,
before I sing the saddest part,
the final lines and the faintest sounds,
with my eyes closed and my heart open I will tell you
each beautiful thing about you
the magic I see in your bright eyes
the perfect words that describe you
the secrets we know, the memories I saved and kept
and the love you have shown.

Leave me be, let me be!
I am filled with your song, your intense serenade
the happiness in your eyes grips me, seduces me,
the sadness that you bring beckons me,
calls my name, commands me,
and I long for you each day.

Fate gives, time takes,
day breaks.

Better

I recall,

before we parted ways,
before we chose to walk towards our own *"destinies"*
(although, yours might have lead you to something better)
you casually mentioned, or rather, reminded me

that I can only do so much.

Your eyes fondly stared at me as you meant those words
neither to accept hopelessness nor make me feel I'm weak,
but you just knew it'd better come from you
than anyone or anybody else.

Who else knew me too well but you?

Your fingers caressed my ears, brushed my hair,
I closed my eyes; a failed attempt
to conceal brimming tears.

Again, you reminded me
that there are better ones, hundreds out there
who could do so much better
who could think better than I could
who could speak or write better than me—

Then,
you took me in your burning arms,
how else could one say goodbye?

After a decade now,
count ten years back from this exact moment in time,
we were still too young when you said to me:

better ones you'll meet
once we are out of this small obsessive world
when we no longer are confined, defined
but simply noticed.

(silence)
said I. Then we parted.

At this very moment,
(try recounting years again)
I finally realize that you only wanted me
to be content
to know who I truly am—
like how
perhaps, you once knew me that much.

After years of waxing and waning,
no doubt, I tried
knowing for some reason I'll see you again,
anticipating, aching, longing
to tell new stories, ask fond questions,
or admit secrets already forgotten—

Like how I miss you
and every memory of you, so real and surreal
my heart weeps every time.

Only you knew me better.

III

untimely defeat

One Year

Could you count a single year
or do we leave it at that?

Could you cross your fingers
or do you want me to pray?

Could you say you love me now
or do we finally move on?

a view from Euston Road, London

At Werner

Can I melt
right this moment?

Like a
sculpted candle
waxing and waning,
wary of your flickering smile
wanting to caress every inch of you
wallowing in mixed and dazed madness
wafting the air with words
and whispers of desire.

Look at me again.

Lost and Found

I will collect sensations
from simple tables and chairs, doors and windows,
and empty boxes and brittle sticks of chalk,
turpentine, paintbrushes, and pencil cases.

I will collect sentiments and thoughts
from breadcrumbs and undelivered mail,
cups and pots, empty shelves and empty drawers,
faded blankets and tattered shoes.

All these I would do
to find you in every little thing, in every contraption,
and books and records, maps, stars and dreams,
because I sent you away, forgot about you,
and I sadly miss you so much.

IV

eternal repose

I wish to live

Someday,

I wish to live during the 15th century
or perhaps anytime over a hundred years back
as long as I find you there
and meet you when you are young as I am,
wherever you may be looking for me.
Someday, I will live centuries ago
where candles burn longer,
and the night is not day, and the night is silent,
and the houses are wood and stone,
and music is written and sung
like poetry and prayer.

I wish to live during the old times someday,
and I will collect pigments and paint pictures
with blunt paintbrushes and broken glass.
I will search for you wherever you may be
and if I find you, I will ask you one thing,
and you will love me for the rest of your life.

Liberty At Last

Staccato.

Red clouds hovered upon the seamless sky
gleaming arrows rained and sprinted
like fireballs and staggering beams
countless roars, cries, bellows and screams
blended into a chorus of ceaseless grief
heroes and warriors and fearless soldiers
trampled the earth in their dreadful flight
their shields and rusted swords rattled
banners and pennants undulated
with life and death, and life after death.

And I?
I kissed the rumbling ground
sealed my lips with dust, soil, and mud
dug the earth with my numbed hands
waited for the unrest to commit suicide
and I prayed for silence to conquer the land.

And as the last arrow flung itself across the sky
before my eyes dimmed and my soul lost grip
I saw your face and loved you for the last time.

The British Museum

A Sounding Vow

In times of loss
or hopelessness,
belligerence or confusion,
believe in love.

Where it lies dormant
it still breathes,
pulsating like the tender heart
in your bosom where it lies.

When love hides it only wants you to seek,
when you hide, love only finds you,
know then, that when true love finds you,
you have nothing, nowhere to hide.

Like you, My Love,
you find refuge in my heart,
you fill my chalice, you consecrate my body
you are proof that dreams are divine,
despite our world's uncertainty.

But nonetheless, I am certain
and I love you,
shall I declare it again and again,
for above the many ways we so fondly express it
there is no simpler way to make it a sounding vow,
and in such simplicity I want your very heart to know
that, I prayed for you as you prayed for me
that, you exist both in dreams and reality
that, once and forevermore
I love you
by all means—
bring me, take me,
kiss me, want me,
love me.

Deliver Me

From the darkness that I see
Whenever I close my eyes
And the nightmares that seduce me
To abandon the past and flee
From the selfishness of the night
And the ominous light of dead stars
From the raveling of prayers
And wishes, rants and regrets
And the absence of sound.

Deliver me from the past
And refuse to grant me
The promise of tomorrow's sunrise
For I, too, am afraid
To witness your sudden flight.

In Prayer and Love

She will pray for you

remember your name and smile

before her eyes dim.

Bury the Dead

I stripped off your mystic skin
and exposed your flesh—bare and bland.
I gasped secretly and denied my face of expression
as I seized the last tiny speck of yearning for you
within me and purged it out of my system.

This is not an act of desperation.
This is a test.
And, I tell you, I passed.
I finally severed you from my body.
And, at last, I revert to my pristine form
without any trace of you in my skin, in my bloodstream,
or in my heart

      my mind

         my words

            my past

               my life.

Crossing Over

It stood in front of the walls of time
opaque as they are, these walls
stood their ground, stood as close
as if anticipating, waiting
for its lifeless caress.

Will it not be held back,
will it not be stopped from breaking loose?
Its hand wavers and hankers,
eyes shut, one cannot breathe,
where are you, my love?

Where are you, my love?
when it is bound to break these walls,
one step closer, and it is gone
where are those hands of yours,
pull me now, bring me back!

It stood in front of the walls of time
opaque as they are, like those eyes
I resist, I stand my ground
only because of you,
now, hold my hand, see me through.

The Penitent Flame *

Look at me, I beg of you,
show me the painful beauty of your face,
and grant me the pleasure of a flickering candle,
and only I shall reflect your peace.

Speak, my love, I beg of you,
tell me the secret behind unspoken words,
soothe me with the sound of your cracking voice.
And I shall fill your room with songs.

Tell me the meaning of penitence
for I do not know what moves me,
what thrills and compels my heart
to lovingly watch you in your solace.

* after Georges de La Tour
  Madeleine aux deux flammes (1638-1643)

Death of Memory *

The mysterious darkness behind you
transforms into a wall concealing your body
from unwarranted gazes and curious eyes.
The empty stage reveals your illuminated flesh—
you neither move nor open your jaded eyes,
and I fear most that I shall be too late
to save you from your ill fate
from your pen's blade and your stranger's hatred

The frozen tips of your fingers timidly touch
the cold, deadened face of the floor,
and your lips—ah, those lips that only I love!
I can kiss no more

---

* after Jacques-Louis David
  La Mort de Marat (1793)

THE RAFT *

The amber sky defied the request of the olive sea
in her ravaging attempt to soothe the plea of souls
waiting tirelessly for some land to claim their unrest.

As if to tease their hankering eyes and arms,
as if to prolong their breath of hope,
illusions of spurious ships befell their curiosity.

And you, you waited for the raft to meet the shore,
your eyes pinned to the far and empty space
and you prayed that I pray for your safe return
and you gripped the edge of the raft in panic
and you calmed your raging heart after each attack
and you whistled fervently to hide your distress
and you heard the wailing of people around you
and you recalled the last words you said to me
and you longed to pull me into your burning arms
and you prayed that I pray for your safe return.

---

* after Théodore Géricault
  Le Radeau de la Méduse (1818-1819)

I now see

Dust, air, light, dreams
tempestuously swirl before me
and with my very own eyes
I now see your body,
I now see your face, those eyes,
those lips that once tormented me,
seducing me into the unknown!
Returning from purgatory!

While I wait for tears
to wet my eyes, blur my vision,
you longingly take me into your arms
you press my body against your chest,
you seize my heart with such burning passion
I can never so faithfully describe until now,
then we gasp for air, you and I,
we drown our fantasies, lies and promises,
we hold on so tightly once and for all
and then
you close your eyes.

Impossible.

I do not love you anymore.

V

eulogies
before
departure

I will write my own Journal

I came across a journal
that unsparingly stitched stories about you
and I did nothing about it
but asked myself if they were all true.

How could you find someone new
six days after our six years
and act as if you have forgotten
the person you have shared your tears?

How could you kiss a lover
and deny the promises you have made
during our enduring summer
and contrived to starve your heart?

How could you have planned a conspiracy
while I happily gave up my ambition
for the love of your smile and arms around me?
I refuse to accept them as illusions.

I will write my own journal
and selfishly speak of you and me,
Perhaps you'll come across it one of these days
My only request is

                    please remember,

                    me.

You are a writer

You are a writer
and I am nothing to you—
I am not a paragraph, not a line,
not a word, not a syllable,
not even a sound.
But even in your poetry
you put blanks and spaces.
Perhaps, I'd like to think,
I'm one of those spaces
in between your words.

Sobriquet

Eyes, how they seize a gaze,
linger in the mind like smoldering orbs

Fingers, how they stick to skin,
puncture stains deeper than bloody tattoos

Lips, how they press against another's,
leave traces of words and sweet wounds

A name, how it spells out thoughts,
repeats like a song, a prayer, a plea

A name, how it sounds

a name, how it is spelled

a name, how it is peculiar

a name, how it matches mine

a name, I will never forget.

Two Worlds Apart

The dawn breaks
again,
tears two worlds apart—
day from night,
light from dark,
lip from lip,
reality from reality,
you from me.

There's thunder
in your arms,
lightning in your wide eyes,
and a catastrophe
gushing out of our hearts.

Tell me
when will we meet
and mend again?

10:58 a.m. at Hauptbahnhof, Frankfurt, Germany

VI

imaginary places

Extra Baggage

One hundred and twenty or thirty
pounds, not quid, but Great British pounds
just to live a late-blooming jet-setter's dream!
From Heathrow to Frankfurt to Tallinn, Estonia,
from Tallinn to Munich et après Charles de Gaulle à Paris,
et puis Gare de Lyon à Londres, via Eurostar.

Six hours earlier:
even charged my phone in advance,
I quit sleep, I quit breakfast,
instead snacked on twenty or fifty words per minute.

Please, please, I badly need your help!
Then she weighed my baggage and she shook her head:
Fifty pounds. No. Let me ask,
how much for an extra bag?
One hundred and twenty or thirty
pounds, not quite, but you're 26 minutes late
(probably count 4 seconds more and counting...)

Please, please, I sorely need to fly!
Then she weighed my baggage and she shook her head:
You need to run. Now. I said,
you seriously need to run!
One hundred and twenty or thirty
seconds, not minutes, in Big Ben's time.
I took my chances, now don't just leave me behind!

"Für Ihre (meine) Sicherheit"

Yes, I met an angel,
she shook her head, but she let me through.
I almost cried but she understood
took her chances, took my baggage, she did save me
One hundred and twenty or thirty
pounds, no extra costs, no hidden charges
just 26.4 kilos of extra baggage

saved me the world.

Inconsistent Time Zones

For some people
in this bulbous globe of winding clocks
two time zones exist.
One is here, the other is there,
one is day, the other is night (or almost),
one is ten minutes past nine p.m.
and the other,
ten minutes past five,
so early in the morning (like now).

The two
never actually meet
but only chase each other
or exchange horizons and stars
or messages across the universe.

This is reality,
or maybe, it's not,
when it feels like a dream
to wake up in your arms for seven days,
sunrays piercing through the blinds
alighting gently on my cheeks
where your beautiful face hides
and rests at the same time.

For me,
between "real" and "unreal"
between "here" and "there"
between "you" and "me"
I know there's only one time,
one chance—

the moment I first saw you.

One Night

The world is too big.
I can't reach the other side.
It seems impossible.

But one night,
I found you on my bed,
I felt the tight grip of your hand.
And we whispered words
nobody could ever hear.
And we flew across the sky
across the sea and far away.
And we discovered parts of the world
nobody has ever seen.
And we took photographs
of us smiling, laughing.
And we counted days,
questions, words and numbers,
and found us in each other's arms.

Tomorrow,
I'll finally reach the other side of the world.
You'll take me there—
to your bed, this time.
And we shall settle in each other's arms.

Supermoon Getaway

Oh, lovely long moonlit weekend, why soon pass?
Why soon fade away and seep into piles of memories?
Waning like the moon, like a sweet song, a duet, a kiss,
we met, we laughed, we swept this city in a breeze...

We playfully followed each other's dreamy trail
under the moon, under the spell of a childish fairytale,
then we silently, secretly watched each other's move,
Oh, *je ne sais quoi!* Let time pass, let time prove.

Tell me a secret

Tell me a secret.
And my lips will touch your ear
like a feather, like a flower,
and I will sing you a song.
Then your eyes will look at me
Oh so lovingly.

Where do you keep your secrets?
In your silly dreams, perhaps,
or your sarcasm and sincerity—
I'd like to know.
And I will listen very carefully
to your breath and your heartbeat
because I know I am there,
and you love me everywhere.

Tartu

I've never seen anything like this before,
this glowing afternoon of bliss
under the sheets and over the rainbow
your quirky jokes soon I'll miss.

I've never felt like this before,
no wonder my heart couldn't believe
this day may never come again
what happens next after we leave?

Tartu, minu
kauge kodu, õnnelik koht
tervislik retsept
on suvi.

Time Travel

She sat comfortably on the sidewalk
while her teary eyes observed colors passing by
her breathing heaved under the humid weather
then she laughed and coughed and calmed down.

She reached inside her pocket
her dry hands gently brushed the chafed fabric,
suddenly remembered nothing was there,
in times like these not even magic dust exist.

As I met her eyes she started guessing
her fingers twitched her eyebrows raised
with one blink her tears glowed and evaporated,
and my lamenting heart melted under her gaze.

She managed to pull a piece of paper
as I feigned a smile,
she was beautiful, her heart longed for love
With one blink, she was young again.

Journey to the wilderness

Today,
I learned a few simple things.

I learned how my fingers can cross
and carefully write a letter,
even with my eyes firmly closed,
as long as my heart is open.

I ate some fresh green leaves,
that's what they call salad,
and learned how to slow down
and pause to see
how beauty sits around me.

Then, at last, I sang two songs,
and for the first time I learned
to listen to every word I sing
simply telling me how life goes on
even if you're gone,
without asking or knowing why,
my prayers do reach the sky.

Summer School

We went to this little city
and walked the seemingly empty streets
little did we know
who, what, where, and why
whoever comes, whatever comes.

We met in this ülikooli
and learned its words and street signs
little did we know
who, what, where, and why
and how to make our two weeks last.

We fell in love in this little city
and shared its streets with strangers like us
little did we know
who, what, where, and why—
do we really have to say goodbye?

VII

earthly sojourns

Reversing Summer

Summer started
and I was waiting impatiently
for some gray clouds
to pour cold rain over me
and drench my delusions
of desire.

I remember
how the cold night reversed summer
and how the stars realigned
to grant me a singular chance
to consummate a love affair
that never really happened.

First Snow

White and delicate
but unlike a feather, unlike a flower,
unlike the little secrets that we tend to keep,
it hushes the bellowing wind
and carelessly falls into
the bosom of this city.

I will not write about the bitter cold,
or frozen hearts and hearts of stone
like how others write so austere,
instead
I will long for his kiss,
the sun, the midday star,
his burning light I will miss.

Instead,
I will thank the heavens,
and the hands of fate in this lifetime
for this one chance to see
such yonder, stark yet sublime.

Instead,
I will selfishly write
until I remember my self again,
from losing love, as everything goes
save for this faithful pen.

Stranger

Stranger, your face you dare show
In front of me, beneath the moon,
And I am unguarded, unarmed,
Vulnerable to your touch
That sting like desire—
Inch by inch you seize
Every part of me
As if I am submitting
Myself to you like mad.

Stranger, I know you crave in the dark,
Your heart is invisible to me,
As you strangle me
And all I can do is keep my eyes shut
For I do not want to lay my sight
Upon your sudden departure.
You will leave me exactly where you found me
And even the wounds you have caused me
You will take them all away,
Leave nothing behind,
Neither your footprints nor a kiss.
You will leave nothing for me to remember—

You
And your unexpected visit
To my world, mine alone.
You are a stranger.

Look

I see curving shades of peach, tan, flesh, and brown
your skin glows under the luminosity of daylight

under the incandescent radiance of the afternoon sun

beneath the glittering lamps of the evening sky
your staring eyes twinkle with countless sparks

under the countless stars pinpricking the darkest night

your honeyed lips curve from dimple to dimple
promising the sweetest sounds, the sweetest kisses

under my daydreaming gaze you smiled unassumingly

your scent wafts and whirls like a magic spell
of morning air, childhood memories, secret recipés

under and over, above and beyond, over and over.

Then I composed myself, cupped my melting heart
lifted my shoulders, lifted my gaze, lifted my foot

You curiously looked at me still looking at you
for a single moment I waited.   Then I walked away.

Who knows how we may see each other again?

Untamed Vanity

You stand proud
blinded in front of a gasping crowd
your palms facing their beaming eyes
your fingers dancing, combing your hair
your feet prancing, lifting your weight
your soul gyrating, evading the shackles
in front of a thrusting mob
you lead a chorus of bewilderment
and impress delusion on their innocence.

You conjure willful acts of suicide
concealed in sheaths of seduction
your palms, stained with blood, gesture wildly
your numbed fingers restrict your reach
your feet, engraved with bruises, twinge madly
your blinded soul forces and releases its grip
beyond the rhythm, the music seduces incessantly
and you leapfrog into the beating night
without meeting the face of light.

I am yours

If you want to—
you can love me
you can say every sweet word and melt my heart
you can watch me while I sleep and paint my dreams
you can think of me every minute and every second
and you can love me
I am yours.

If you want to—
you can hurt me
you can fool me and break my heart
you can send me away or leave me alone
you can forget my name and ignore the past
and you can hate me
I am yours.

Falter

I do not understand
why I have to meet you now
why you have to come into my life
so suddenly without warning me
that you might make me weak
and fall again and again.

I do not understand
what is it that I see in your eyes
you tell me everything with your gaze
you tell me everything with your smile.
but still I do not understand
why I have to answer
why I have to give
My everything in return.

Now you've changed me—
For once in my life
it's not me anymore
it's all about you—

how you make me happy

how you ease the pain

how you make me falter

how you love me.

How you love me.

Silence and Madness

You're standing in front of me
and I anticipate quietly
that our eyes meet without intention.
I can hear the words that you speak
clear, like they were meant for me
And your laughter echoes
within these four walls
that imprison me.
I don't know how they hold me captive
And yet they imprison you not.

The more I listen, the more I keep
losing track of time and myself.
The more I hear you, the more I forget
who I am and who I am not to you.
The more I watch your lips move
with every sound escaping,
The more I am lured to madness—
the kind of madness that stops me
from touching your face,
the kind of madness that makes me
realize that your eyes show age
And content from somebody's embrace,
happiness not from me,
never in a thousand years.

VIII

into
sacrosanct
dreams

At an empty corner

At an empty corner of the ceiling
kept hidden in the dingy basement
guarded by a sturdy wooden door
and its rusting cables and chains,
I cowered upside down
And gritted my nails patiently.
The furtive walls kept vigil,
suspicious of my every sudden move;
for every scant movement that I attempt
unsettles their secret boredom.
This meaningless torture perhaps I deserve
as I had already forgotten my name,
and I had long forgotten the features of my face,
the sound of my own voice, the taste of sunlight
on my pale cheeks and numbed lips,
since you deserted me tonight.

But all is not lost.
Because the truth is, I know—
the moment I open my eyes after this endless night,
you will return.

How long do I have to hold my breath?

Whenever you are in the same room as me
or in the same place, such as this—

I hold my breath and make no sound
I dare not look or think at all
I dare not move lest I distract you
perhaps, it's better this way.

For now,
I am content
just knowing, simply knowing
that we are restless under the same placid sky
we look at the same Moon, Venus, Mars
we breathe the same air, the same plasma
and yes, we share the same lifetime.

Now,
while you're still here in the same room as me
while we're still in the same lonely sea of Stars
by all means I will prove my strength,
I will resist, by all means I will remain calm,
by all means I will not drown.

Just when love inundates the realm of emotions
I only think of one thing and one thing only—

How long do I have to hold my breath?

Mirror

You held your breath,
sat calmly on the cold cement,
looked at him with your eyes closed,
stared intently at his laughing eyes
glanced at his playful hands
observed his fingers move.

Without a doubt you loved him so
but you never told him yet
and, perhaps you might never tell
anyone, any single thing at all,
but the secret is, I know.

Now, in front of this mirror,
you look at your eyes wide open,
you stare at the pale expression of your face,
you glance at the hazy room behind you,
you observe your burning heart.

How can you hurt if you cannot feel?

How can you regret if you cannot love?

Look,

I am a mirror
I am invisible to your eyes
but let me tell you, for what it's worth
My love for you never dies.

I falter again

Behind closed doors
behind makeshift walls and panels
right at the backstage that extends
as far as our eyes can see
as far as the light can bounce
we met surreptitiously
we whispered secretly
we imagined the tempting glare
of spotlights and spectators
the chilling cold of the empty stage
where we'll one day kiss
but now we move on.

We crafted ingenious ways to hide
while we recited lines and sounds
I played music you liked to hear
you sang songs and I carefully listened
and we spent moments that burn.

Why are we doing this?
Is it by chance or by choice?
Your eyes look at a distant shore
While my sight is fixed on the future.
If we did meet by some silly chance
and we know we are making believe
stealing glances, making sounds
why then, why do we still choose?

Who will believe us when we say
we chose right? we chose wrong?
We are alone but together we're free
in our imagined time and space
in our peculiar affair, silly choice,
but now we move on.

But how do we choose?
I know the answer but I cannot move
I falter again in your gripping arms
With your eyes, your smile, I falter again.

In My Room

In my room—
where I dump words that never sound,
where I see the blue walls turn
to sky and falling leaves in my dreams,
where I feel the parquet under my feet
melting into earth and piercing my skin
gently like sand and soil,
where I throw myself into the sea of mist
and sheets of wind,
where I hurl every breath
and haul sentiments and impressions
and keep them in my basket,
where I retrieve colors of mocha,
peach, skin, gray, white and azure
from the empty closet,
where I recall strange sounds like words
and strange words like noise
coming from the village outside,
where I translate movement to music
and stillness to painted pictures,
where whenever I am awake
I barely notice the passing of time,
and whenever I am asleep
I dream of doors and windows—
I sit at an empty corner, stop moving,
and remember you.

You stood behind the door,
and I at the other side,
patiently watching out for the first sound
I'll hear from your side.

You knocked,
and calmly asked me to let you in
as I held my breath
and consulted my heart for a response.

I hesitated for a few moments,
clutched my hands,
and finally
opened the door.

Two years.

IX

hallucinations

Murky Past

You amuse me.
How it seems so easy for you to forget about me,
how you conveniently erase memories,
just to prove you have moved on.

You amuse me.
How you easily slip from memory to memory,
how you treat our past like fallen petals,
and just let them wither away.

You amuse me.
How you carefully, cleverly choose your sentences,
how you use your words, your playful mind,
just to amuse me all over again.

You used to bathe in the past and drink its spirit
night and day you sing tirelessly about madness
and in your drunkenness you never noticed
how silently, I stood by
how silently, I dressed your wounds
as though you did everything on your own,
as if you recovered, as if you moved on
without me, without my hand.

You amuse me.
How you speak as if you never knew
that once in your murky past
I did love you.

Standing Ovation

What's in a name?

Otto:
you thought of her with much spite,
yet with much love.
You can never deny it but you saw me too
you saw me when I saw you,
we'll never know who first saw who.
I wouldn't have surrendered
if it weren't for your clandestine eyes.
If it weren't for your beckoning heart.

Giuseppe:
tell me again how fresh flowers taste
like flesh or bloody wine
to your lips, sing me another song!
before you break your heart, succumb,
send me a single rose's kiss,
with a name, the name *Givola.*

Basilio:
I was there, whether you knew it
or never,
but when you needed my strength,
my words and hands to hold you,
to carry you through your own battles,
when you sorely wanted me
while the others flee—

I was there. *I was there.*

A disputed *Vladimir* or *Julius Caesar,*
or simply
your allusive namelessness, your highness—
the list of roles and sobriquets continues...
You hide in different names, different faces,
different lights and scaffolding mazes,
while you hid me secretly, selfishly in your
subconscious flights of kisses
and embraces.

Whether I may never get to know you
at all, or see you again,
this is my final act, I tell you, my eulogy,
A Tribute to Innocence.

(Standing ovation)

Still not over.

Still not over.
A phrase so innocuous and empty
that your lips shuddered and your heart
twitched at the thought of it.

Still not over.
A line you keep on repeating to yourself
until your senses become numb
and your reason obscured.

Still not over.
A sad utterance I just came up with
to tell you that my sudden reticence
is your cue to retreat.

Still not over

Still not over—
these words do not mean anything to me,
a phrase so empty
that my lips shuddered at the thought of it.

Still not over—
these words I recall and recite in my head
until the sense of it evades me
and what is left of me are sounds
that I mutter with respite.

Still not over—
these words you just spilled recklessly
to dispel me, confuse me, hurt me,
forget me, leave me alone.

Amongst the Stars

I am afraid.
The last time I saw you was not in a dream
I can vaguely remember, but yes—it was you
my mind will prove what my eyes do believe.

Now I hover amongst the stars
suspended in deep boundless darkness
my mind prowls the sea of glittering sand—
in search of the one thing it will never find.

When I let you go you haplessly fled
you hid so cleverly amongst the heavenly stars
your earthly charm blended in their chorus of light
and your glimmer lingers every sleepless night.

When I let you go you happened to fly
you never said a word but you left a smile
my mind will prove what my heart believes
now I defy the stars in pursuit of a wish—

Once and for all come back to me!
Or I shall take advantage of gravity
I will plunge through the abyss of oblivion
and we shall never see each other again.

First Light

If I wake up,
look at my hands and lift my face,
peek at the gleaming window
between my fingers and see
the empty sheets of clouds,
will I be able to tell apart skies,
shores, latitudes, spaces, places?

If I wake up,
and feel the ebbing December breeze
cold as the damp kiss of morning,
will your smiling eyes greet me again?

Like the brightest day between spring and summer
or the happiest moment of my youthful life,
simply reminding me

that,

life goes on,

love lives on.

X

first light

Morning

Morning,

I feel your sweet, soft breath
lightly touching my pale skin,
as you waft around me
like a scent from my childhood,
like a puff of hugs and kisses
bringing foggy reveries
of sweet things, simple things,
and unfading memories that glow
with each sliver of sunlight,
or each thing
that only you can show.

I love every little bit of you
every strand of your glowing hair,
every speck of your glistening skin,
but I love your touch even more—
you caress my heart with warmth,
with each promise that you bring,
you embrace me with tenderness,
you whisper, you speak, you sing.

Your happiness is forever young,
and I feel you smiling beside me,
and I trust to meet you,
to fall for you,
to lovingly adore you as I wake up
from a long, seemingly endless night
of deep, deep slumber.

Morning,
wake me up and kiss me please,
so I may let me forget, let me go,
and learn to live again.

Today

Today, I will open my hands
and receive.

I will open my eyes
and understand
that things happen for a reason
that the world is still beautiful
that love is true, love is real.

And today, just for once,
I'll thank myself for who I am
and gladly, happily let me be
open my hands and let go
open my eyes and accept
that love is true,
love is real.

The world is still beautiful.

I flung myself into the open sky

I flung myself into the open sky
and clasped my hands above my head
and opened my eyes as wide as the sea
and took a deep breath
effortlessly.
I am a child, a playful child
my days are short, and my nights last long
but there's no difference when I'm in a dream
I'm awake anyhow,
I transform at whim.

Before the setting sun, before dusk dawns
let me dance again, let me tell a story
let me collect leaves, fallen twigs and branches
I love, I stumble
I believe in second chances.

Outside

The streets are colder, even wider

alleys run deeper than surreptitious whispers

of bygone couples and dazed lovers

When I look at you

When I look at you I only see hope
despite the dimming world
and the silent darkness around me.

When I look at you I only see hope
despite the clutter in my mind
and the noise that surrounds me.

Look at me.
Just look at me and tell me—
how do I love you?
When you are not made of words,
and your light inspires me,
and I can only feel your warmth.

But how do I love you?
What do you see when you close your eyes?
For whenever I sleep I see your face
and whenever I close my eyes I see the same.

But how do I love you?
How often should I say your name?
For whenever I say your name I make no sound
and whenever I miss you I say it out loud.

But how do I love you?
How rarely should I speak about us?
For whenever I speak I say too much
and whenever I'm with you I lose those words.

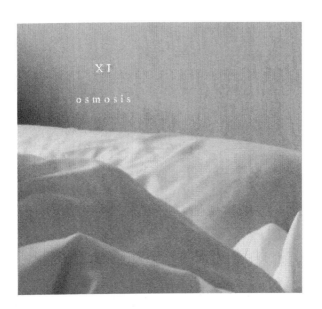

XI

osmosis

If I commit

If this
confused
convoluted
covert affair
with you
with me, between the two of us,
is supposed to happen according to the stars
of fate and fortuity,
or suppose that it must work
according to our cosmic desires,
libidinal or ethereal—
pray admit and profess the truth:
if we are meant to meet and permeate
each other's skin and bones,
each other's soul and element,
why does it sting like pins and needles
why does it smother my heart
why does it scathe like hell
why does it suffocate

why does it?

to please you
to kiss you
to want no other body
no other one, else it's you

why does it—
if I commit?

I keep myself awake

I keep myself awake
whenever you're beside me
because I find peace
and I am content
just watching you sleep.

I keep myself awake,
let you sleep by my side,
let you dream about us
while I think about you
and thank you secretly.

When I look at you
night becomes a sunny day,
and I smile and cry
because you are nowhere else
but here right beside me.

Secretly, I kiss you—
and patiently wait for dawn
to see your bright eyes,
and hear your voice—
to know the reason I'm alive,
to love you one more day.

Without Words

I can tell how you feel—

When you are happy
your eyes smile while you speak
your fingers tinker with your hair
and your laughter completes my day.

When you are sad and you feel alone
you talk too little or you don't talk at all
you shrug your shoulders and silently stare
at the emptiness that only you can see.

You don't need words at all
it's clear to me when you feel something
I don't need to guess when you're in love
even without words, I know.

But how can I tell you without words
I am happy every time you smile
I am happy when you let me hold your hand
and my heart leaps and falls like mad.

I am sad when your day turns gray
I am sad when you rant behind closed doors
and it hurts me because I've always been here
but you don't hear words, you don't feel.

Now, how can I tell you without words
without the courage to make you understand
that I feel for you, and my heart wants you,
and I love you even without words.

Leap Day Musings

Take me to a place
where no one else has been,
not even you, not even your sight,
not even the warmest day
or coldest sunlight.

Wherever that is,
as long as you're there,
or as far as you can remember,
take me once, just lead me,
and then, set me free.

No wonder
you're tired of counting days
or following the dance of the seasons.
You run too fast and love too little;
your heart's a maze, your love's a riddle.

Osmosis

I was looking forward to the next stop
My eyes closed, my mind open, my feet apart
not a single distraction could keep me
not even the dazzling lights that went past
not even the rumbling of roads and highways
not even the thought of you not waiting for me
because I have something to say.

I had never felt so alone as I waited there
patiently, intently, among the stoic crowd
not a single distraction could move me
not even the gray skies and pouring rain
not even the impending distress of sorts
not even the panic I felt deep in my heart
because I have something to say.

All was a blur, in slow, slow motion
everywhere was gray, murky gray
lights collided with the mist and the rain
everything sounded like heartbeats rushing
everything sounded like sirens and noise
everything recurred like scenes from a movie
rewinding and playing, rewinding and playing.

I pushed.

You pulled.

You pushed.

I pulled.

I want you more than words can say.
I want you more than words can say.

XII

vows of love

Smile Lines

She took a long, intimate pause
before she lifted her sweet, sweet face
then took small and gentle steps
towards the sunny lawn,
towards him, smiling like never before.

He held her hand,
lovingly watched her eyes glitter
with awe, visible smile lines,
and pearly tears,
as he waited for the right moment
to respond with a breathless kiss,
sealed with a silent prayer.

Do you still remember
the moment our praying lips parted
when we bid us farewell?
How I went to the sea and drank
its mellifluous laments and lullabies,
how I painted the stars, wrote your name
across the sky, sang for you and slept
for a hundred years of solitude,
how I, finally, let go?

Now,
before our smile lines show age
and fade like memories,
take her hand,
touch his face,
look

I never stopped loving you,
and I will, forevermore,
love the happiness in your eyes.

What is need?

What is need?
Tell me.
Is need entirely different from want?
Or is it an allusion to uninhibited desire?
You must tell me.
For whenever you persist in my mind,
everything blurs
and I am confused.
I lose the meaning of words
while sentiments compel me to hesitate
whenever you look at me,
whenever your hand touches mine,
or whenever I'm in your arms.

But above all I'm certain
that my body will break if I lose you;
and I will only refuse to recover
until I dispel my desolation
and finally understand
that I want you,
and I need you,
and I love you above all.

I love you a million times more

Because I love you a million times more
I burn my body to exhaustion
because I love you a million times more
I bleed my heart dry
because I love you a million times more
and I love you over and over again
and I will endure my solitude and misery
and I will breathe underwater, beneath the sea
because I love you a million times more
  and I love you over and over again
and my mind cannot contain you
because I love you a million times more
and I will stay and persist
but you will not notice me
and I will invade your mind
but you will not feel that I am here
because I love you a million times more
and I love you over and over again.

And you will ask me questions
but I will not say a word
because I love you a million times more
and I love you over and over again.

Rue Sainte Croix de la Bretonnerie, Paris

Riddle

You run too fast and love too little;

your heart's a maze, your love's a riddle.

Estonian Theatre House, Tartu

XIII

we are mere water

Moonless water, starless sea

In my slumber
the moonless water lustfully crept
over the dark pebbles covering the shore
licked and lapped the hem of my blanket
while my body rolled
and slithered
onto the edge of the bed, the shore,
my hands dipped
into the starless sea.

Stealthily, I waited
for sea monsters
to emerge from the deeps
and strike me hard with pangs of anguish
with ruthless jaws
until I bleed
rip
die
and drift
woefully into oblivion.

But you wake me up
with your burning arms around me
grappling me away from despair,
your lips touching my ears
longingly calling my name in stifled whimpering
with unstoppable tears pouring from your eyes,
your body desperately heaving with courage,
and I suddenly realize
that I am yours completely,
that my heart burns for you,
that I am yours completely,
that I am yours completely.

I Am the Sea

I am the sea
and you are the cold night
you blanket me with awe
and lull me to sleep.

I am the sea
and you are the little drops of water
that make up my entirety
and I am alive.

I am the sea
and you are the wind—
you push me away
and I resist
you stir me into waves
and I lose control
as I unleash bursts
of unceasing grief
to retrieve my sanity.

I am the sea
after the storm,
catching my breath,
drowning your name
deeper and deeper
until I finally consume you
and forget.

2001

an island in Palawan, Philippines

Sea of make-believe

Once more, I entered my room,
this time wide awake,
and the traces of lurid dreams
and delusions have all faded.

I sat on the floor
near the unkempt bed
and waited for something
to happen.

Nothing moved
except my fingers that twitched restlessly.
My eyes paced the confines of the room
and I forced my mind to respond.

You never arrived.
Not even a figment of you,
or a feeble sound
to announce your return.

And I sat still
waiting patiently for the sea of make-believe
to flood my room until I drown,
then you will save me again.

Stargazing Cancer

I knew this time would come.

My eyes have seen it and I believed.

The stars revealed your name
as I whispered sweet incantations and deep breaths
beneath the moon, beneath the changing sky
for countless middays and midnights I sought
to see your face, to find your dreams,
to match your stars with mine
but I never found you.

Then without you, I shall set sail
through darkness, nightmares and tempting visions
let my dreams stretch as sails on a powerful mast
and my heart a compass pulsating with light.

Amidst the boundless ocean of vague realities
even without your hand I take the plunge
I will never drown for I am water
and I bring life, I am.

I Am Cancer
I am not a single star but a sea
I am my wishes and dreams, I am a mystery
I am love, I love
and I will find you, let it be.

XIV

sariling wika

Hinabing mga alaala *

KJCA

Nagbibilang ako ng mga taon,
kay bilis pala lumipas ng panahon.
Minamadali ako sa bawat paghinga,
akala ko'y nalimot na kita.

Naghihintay sa paglipas ng panahon,
sabihin sa 'kin, nasaan ka na ngayon?
Nanaginip, nanahimik sa bawat araw,
sigla ng kahapon, hindi na matanaw.

Hindi naman masamang ako'y mangarap
sa bawat gabi, ikaw ang hanap-hanap
hindi naman masama kung aking isipin
ang 'yong puso'y minsan naging akin.

---

* Woven memories

Vigan, Ilocos Sur, Philippines

Kamay sa aking pisngi *

KJCA

Binabalot ng malamlam na liwanag ang dapithapon
ngunit hindi man lang mabawasan ang tingkad ng paligid
sa halik ng naglalagablab na araw na kay lamig sa paningin,
sa ilalim ng ating nangungulimlim na himpapawid.

Habang nakaupo, inilapag ang mga palad,
huminga ng malalim, ipinikit ang mga mata,
pinagmasdang maigi ang naninibagong kulay ng kawalan
para bang isang taimtim na dasal, binulong ang 'yong pangalan.

Tikom ang mga palad na nanalangin at nangamba
sa iyong paglisan, sa aking pangungulila.
Sa 'di kalayuan, nangibabaw ang makukulay na alaala
hanggang dito, hanggang ngayo'y hinahanap-hanap pa rin kita.

Habang nangingilid ang mga luhang 'di mo napapansin,
binasag ng 'yong ngiti ang katahimikang namamagitan sa atin
iyong palad sa aking pisngi, muling inamin ang nadarama
iyong kamay sa aking puso, muling ipinangako ang pagsinta.

Huwag mong kalilimutan ang init ng aking yakap,
pagmasdan mo na lamang ang pagtigil ng bawat araw,
isantabi ang pangamba, palipasin ang paglalim ng gabi,
alalahanin ang dampi ng aking kamay sa iyong pisngi.

---

* Palm on my cheek

*Baha 1**

JEFFREY NOEL C. AGUSTIN

Parang drogang nagpapatulog sa akin.
Ang isip, nilulunod at tinatangay
Ninanakaw ang pandinig ko't paningin.
Nawawala sa sarili, walang malay.

Tila isang oyayi'ng himig ng ulan
na nagpatahimik sa boses ng lupa.
Mga nasira, patungo sa kawalan
sa salaming baha na di humuhupa.

Langit ay umiiyak ng luhang bagyo.
Lupa'y lasing sa tubig baha at putik
na umaapaw sa baga't ugat nito.
Lason din ang tubig 'pag sobrang humalik.

Ang mga anino na umaaninag
Parang tintang humalo sa mga alon
Na gustong makipaglaro, nagtatawag.
Ngunit alam ko ang pahamak niyang baon.

Tila paruparong bihag ng ulan.
Di makalipad, pakpak ay walang silbi.
di makatakas sa kulungan ng tubig.
Hinahanap ang langit araw at gabi.

Tulad ng bituka ng isang halimaw.
Walang hangin sa karagatan ng bubog.
Sa loob nito'y ilalim di matanaw.
Ika'y lalamunin, kumukulogkulog.

Malalaman mo na lang na patay ka na
habang lumulutang sa hukay ng tubig.
Nakahiga, ika'y tulala sa taas.
Suminghap na ang hininga sa'yong bibig.

Panalangin mo'y makita ang liwanag.
Ngunit paraiso'y nilibing sa ulap.
Ika'y malulula, katawang binuwag.
Pipikit. Isang pundidong alitaptap.

Baha II

Walang kasing itim, sobrang dilim.
Walang makita, walang marinig.
Ang inaasam asam ang pilak mong lamig.
Kapalaran ay nakatali sa tahanang binaha--
lahat ng kasama ko'y tinangay na't nilunod.
Nagiisa't nalulugmok; naisin ma'y walang mata para lumuha.

Nililok akong ganito.
Katawan ay 'di nasawi ngunit pagkatao'y nahati.
Ang bagyo ng buhay marahil ang naglayo
Sa 'ting dal'wa para humanap ng iba--
Bagong kapares, bagong kasangga.

Kung di man makahanap ng bagong kasama,
habang buhay makukulangan ng saysay.
dahil wala ka na, wala na tayo.
Ngayon ang tanging silbi'y sumalok.
Sa mga sanaw ng kung ano-ano.

Mas mabuti pa'y hukayin na lang ang sariling libing,
Dahil kung wala ka'y ako'y gutom,
hungkag, walang laman
kundi ang patapon-tapong, paapaw-apaw
na mga lunaw at likido.

Kung kaya lang hukayin ang lupa,
at mag-iwan ng balon ng kawalan,
para masaid lahat ng baha at lahat ng tinangay nito
papunta sa alimpuyo ng aking puso
nang walang matirang patak na magtatangay sayo palayo.

Hahagilapin lahat ng aagusin sa kailaliman nito
hanggang sa ika'y matagpuan.

At muling bumalik sa aking piling.

---

* Flood (I & II)

Huling Pagsusulit *

ROLDAN P. PINEDA

Oras ng pagpiga sa utak ng bawat isa
Abala ang lahat na nag-iisip
Naghahagilap ng sagot sa hangin
Ang isa, tinataktak ang panulat
Ang isa pa ay nakatingin sa kawalan
At 'yong isa ay kinukulot ng daliri ang buhok

Pero may isang sandaling ako'y ginambala mo
Nahulog ang iyong mga gamit—
Ang iyong test paper na humihigop ng lamang-utak
Ang iyong asul na sagutang-papel
At ang iyong itim na bolpen
Pinulot ko ang mga iyon at inabot sa iyo

Subalit hindi ko inaasahang
Magtama ang ating mga mata
Nakita ko ang kabuuan ng iyong mukha
May mahinang ngiti sa iyong mga labi
At sa likod ng iyong titig
Namumutawi ang iyong munting pasasalamat

Hindi ako nagsisising pinulot ko
Ang gamit mo na sa akin ay umistorbo
Sapagkat nasilayan ko
Ang mga matang kumiliti sa aking kaibuturan
Ang mga matang may kislap ng bituin sa gabi
Ang mga matang may musikang nagpakalma sa ligalig at sawi

Iyon ang huling pagsusulit natin
At iyon ay hindi na mauulit muli.

––––––––––––––––––––

* Final Exam

Waiting Shed

K A T R E E N A   R A M O S

Nandito ulit ako sa waiting shed.
Naghihintay. Nag-aabang.
Umaasang, pagkatapos ng lahat ng nangyari..
babalik ka sakin.

Ito na ang huling araw na gagawin ko 'to.
Kapag hindi ka pa rin dumating, titigil na ako.
Hindi ko na kaya. Suko na.
Bibitawan na kita.

Dito sa waiting shed na 'to tayo unang nagkakilala.
Unang nagtawanan. Unang nagkwentuhan.
Pinasaya mo ako nung mga araw na malungkot ako.
Ganun din ako sa'yo.

Sa'yo ko unang narinig ang mga katagang
Gusto kitang mahalin at *Mahalaga ka sa'kin*
Pero anong nangyari?
Bigla kang nawala na parang bula..

Sinabi mong ako ang laman ng bawat *ngayon* mo.
Na handa kang ibigay ang *ngayon* mo para sakin.
Atensyon. Oras. At panahon.
Ngunit iniwan mo pa rin ako.

Marahil natapos na ang *ngayon* na tinutukoy mo.
Sana'y naisip kong kailanman
Hindi ako magiging parte ng *bukas* mo.
Na darating ang panahong kalilimutan mo ako.

Iniwan ko ang isang bagay
Na matagal ko nang pinanghahawakan
Para sa'yo.
Dahil umasa ako sa'yo. Sa atin.

Nakakalungkot isiping dito tayo magtatapos.
Pagkatapos ng lahat ng ginawa ko para sa'yo
Nagawa mo pa rin akong saktan.
Ayoko ng ganito.

Gusto kitang makasama kaya ako nandito ngayon.
Hindi ko pinapansin ang lamig dahil sa lakas ng ulan.
Basta ang alam ko..
kailangan kita sa tabi ko.

Sana kahit papano, kailanganin mo rin ako ulit.
Sana maisip mo rin ako.
Sana magawa mo rin akong mahalin at sana..
Sana ako ang piliin mo.

Isang oras na ang nakalipas.
Wala akong napala kundi basang damit at sapatos.
Hindi ka dumating.
At hindi ka na darating.

Tumayo ako.
Kahit mahirap, nagawa kong umalis.
Pinilit kong tanggapin ang katotohanan.
Kahit masakit, tinalikuran kita.

Binitawan ko ang pag-asang babalik ka sakin.
Naglakad ako sa gitna ng ulan
Kasama ang lahat ng sakit sa dibdib ko.
Ang isang bagay na 'di ko magawang bitawan.

Hindi pa ko nakakalayo nang may dumaang jeep.
Tumigil sa tabi ko kaya't sumakay ako
Dala ang lahat ng sama ng loob dahil sa'yo
At sa ginawa mo sakin.

Sa ilang saglit, napalingon ako sa waiting shed
At ikaw ang nakita ko. Mag-isa.
Nakaupo at tila naghihintay.
Nag-aabang . .

. . . sa wala.

Limang Mundo*

JENNICA CASTILLO

Makita ka lamang
masilayan mga mata
buo na ang araw
ngiti sa labi'y matamis na

Mundo ay tumitigil
pag ikaw ay lumalapit
ni hindi makakibo
huwag ka sanang magagalit

Di naghahangad ng sobra
sa pag-ibig na parang karera
tanggap na sa puso mo ay
hindi naman ako ang nauna

Luha'y di na sana tumulo
kung sa'kin pinagkatiwala ang puso
ngunit anong aking gagawin
kung ang palaging sambit ay siya pa rin?

Limang mundo ang ating pagitan
ngunit handa ko itong ipaglaban
limutin na ang 'yong nakalipas
pansinin naman pag-ibig kong wagas

Kung maaari lang talaga sana
kung kaya ko lang dayain ang tadhana
iuukit ating mga pangalan
papawiin ang pait ng nakaraan

Nararapat bang ako ay umasa pa
sapat na bang ako ay iyong nayakap na
ilusyon lang ba ang init sa'yong mata
ligtas na bang sabihin na mahal na kita?

---

* Five Worlds

Coda

Fisherman

JANINE DEL ROSARIO

Like a fisherman
you gently reel me in.
You feed me with bait
the kind which I can't refuse.

And I fight your hook and line
I fight hard and with passion
fully aware that when you win,
I will be worse than dead.

Suddenly you let go.
I breathe a sigh of relief.
finally
I can live.

I feel you again
and you reel me in hard
you don't give up.
Nor will I.

I will fight for my freedom,
the liberty I have always craved for.
No matter how painful it may be,
I will struggle for my escape.

Like a fisherman, you reel me in.
Like a fish, I will fight for me.

Epilogue

Imaginary places are not always far-fetched. If we simply choose to go "there", we are then looking at a destination—that moment and place in the near or distant future palpable enough to reach.

True enough, imagining and going places almost always bring me to experiencing poetry in many different forms, sounds, and images. Upon reaching each destination—that secluded beach, that dilapidated house, that revered sanctum, even that busy street I pass every day—I always gasp for words, hardly ever seizing the best possible way to describe how I truly feel.

Strange as this may sound, I truly believe that love and poetry exists in every place, no matter where we are or where we want to go. Believe that you will find it; but first choose to go "there".

K J C A

13 September 2012

Revival

For love is something that is often vague,
we define it, but we forget what it means—
it is not simply longing or yearning
or needing somebody to hold your hand;
it means believing, and having faith,
and giving yourself without regretting
and willingly loving without pain.

2012

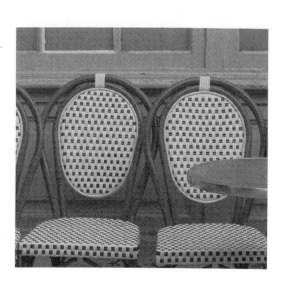

Author's Notes

in Prologue, p8
In 2009, my poetry & photography blog debuted with the question:
'Do you love poetry?'—it aimed to entice readers to think about the
art of love poetry. This book revisits the same question and affirms it in
chorus with other writers.

in Rain Suit Skating, p41 and L.S.S, p36
'Rain Suit Skating' is an anagram of 'Kristian Agustin', which I wrote
in 2002 for our Creative Writing 100 class (University of the Philippines)
under the tutelage of professor Paolo Manalo, Ph.D.
The poem *L.S.S.* is another piece created for the same class. L.S.S. is an
acronym for the urbanism 'Last Song Syndrome'.

in After Twelve Months, p52
An *'umlaut'* is a vowel sound in German (or other Germanic languages)
represented by a ˝ over a vowel. (For example: über, Wörterbuch, für)

in pp72-74
The Penitent Flame, Death of Memory, and *The Raft* is a triptych
inspired by three historical paintings which echoes the movement of art
from Baroque (The Penitent Magdalen) to Neoclassicism (The Death of
Marat) and Romanticism (The Raft of the Medusa).

in Extra Baggage, p82
Quid is a British colloquial term for 'one pound' (or Pounds Sterling).
'Für Ihre Sicherheit' is a phrase that translates as 'For Your Security'
(or Safety), which caught my attention as I boarded a German aircraft.
I added *'meine'* (my) into the phrase for my poem.

in Supermooon Getaway, p87
A *supermoon* occurs when a full/new moon is at its closest to the Earth
during its orbit. This astrological term describes the phenomenological
effect the moon has on the Earth.
'Je ne sais quoi!' is a French phrase/expression that translates literally
as 'I don't know what', a colloquialism of 'I couldn't describe it!'

in Tartu, p91
Tartu is a small city in Estonia, where the 18th Asia-Europe Foundation
University was held in 2012, which I had the opportunity to attend.

in Epilogue, p155
'Imaginary places...' is the opening statement of my MA dissertation
(2012) inspired by Marc Augé's *Non-Places (1995)* and Nicholas Mirzoeff's
The Right to Look (2011).

Deepest thanks to

The avid writers, contributors, and readers who helped shape and animate the collection into a book, from inception until printing (November 2012). Thank you.

Miss LAKSMI PAMUNTJAK, the lovely Indonesian columnist and poet whom I met earlier at the London Poetry Parnassus 2012. She graced this anthology with her poem *Light Matters* right after publishing her new novel, *'Amba',* a revisiting of the story of Amba and Bhisma from The Mahabharata. Her anthology *'Ellipsis'* was one of The Herald UK Books of the Year 2005.

YEN OOI, for welcoming me into her marvelous world of cats (Odin and Freya) and zombies, and above all, for granting us permission to publish *Aquilae* and *Can You.* A talented musician, Yen has had an impressive stint in music touring and management, which includes tours such as the BBC Symphony Orchestra, David Foster & Friends, and the Malaysian Music Awards '97.

JAMES TREMLETT, for sending me his piece *Marenui* whilst adventuring in Turkey (and around Asia), and for his brief e-mail lecture on the Polynesian suffix '-nui' and the Maori article 'te'. He recently finished his studies in geography and ecology at the University of Auckland, New Zealand. We both adore the ocean.

MM MERILO, JANINE DEL ROSARIO, and MARTIN VIDANES, for generously contributing *Captured, Fisherman,* and *CCTV,* respectively, upon the publisher's request. Their works inspire me.

DEAN DA CONCEICAO, a graduate of English Literature from the University of Westminster, London, for assisting in the meticulous editing and 'curating' of all the poems considered for this book.

My family,
Ma and Pa, Jenny my beautiful sister, and younger brother Jeffrey, for all their love. You are the first love of my life.

About the Artist & Author

KRISTIAN JEFF specialises in visual art, graphic design, and film; occasionally writing music and songs, theatre pieces, and poetry. Born in 1984, the Year of the Rat, he considers himself a well-rounded 'Cancerian' who delves into art and poetry as an effective means of self-expression and learning.

He accomplished his Master's degree in Visual Culture at the University of Westminster, London in 2012, after completing his dissertation on 'social media interventions in nation-building and subject formation'. In 2006, he obtained his Bachelor's degree in Art Studies at the University of the Philippines, where he co-founded the *Sirkulo ng mga Kabataang Artista* (or 'Circle of Young Artists') in 2002 and served as its Artistic Director from 2004 to date.

Recent collaborations include: his calligraphy work in *Fishes of Light / Peces de Luz (2013)* by lauded Filipina writer Prof. Marjorie Evasco and award-winning Cuban poet Alex Fleites, and Chinese painter/ink brush calligrapher Ma'am Chua Keng Keng; his libretto of *Ageless Passion (2011)*, a musical with original music by Filipino maestro Ryan Cayabyab; and his calligraphy, logo design and concept art for *Earth.O (2012)*, a transmedia storytelling by London-based Malaysian writers Yen Ooi and Ari Abraham.

WWW.UNIVERSEANDWORDS.COM

BOOK DESIGN, LAYOUT & PHOTOGRAPHS
BY KJCA

Printed in Great Britain
by Amazon